Macroeconomics and Microeconomics for Forex and Currency Traders

Roggie Clark

Continue Learning At Our Website: Roggieclarkbooks.com

Continue exploring educational resources, tools, books, workbooks, and learning materials designed to help readers continue building knowledge and practical skills. Visit: www.roggieclarkbooks.com

Inside you'll find:

- Educational worksheets
- Beginner-friendly guides
- Printable activities
- Companion materials for books and courses

A growing library of educational content for readers, collectors, learners, parents, teachers, and lifelong students.

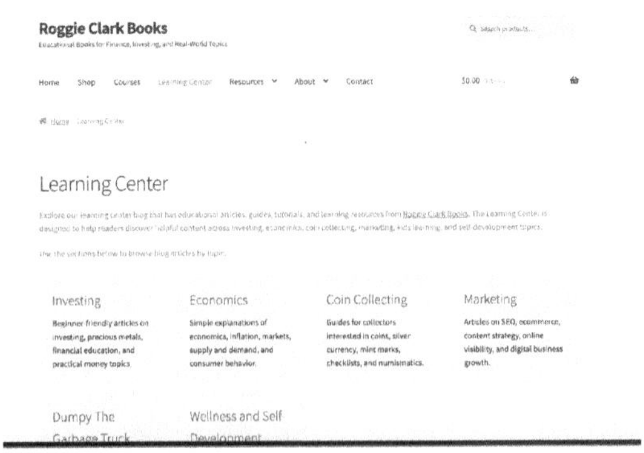

Learn Macro and Micro Economics, With This One Book

Whether you're a student, a professional, or simply someone eager to understand the world around you, this book is your perfect introduction to the fundamentals of micro and macroeconomics.

https://www.amazon.com/Macro-Micro-Economics-Workbook-Beginners-ebook/dp/B0FVPMFX6B

The Strategic Guide to U.S. Mint Gold and Silver Coin Investing

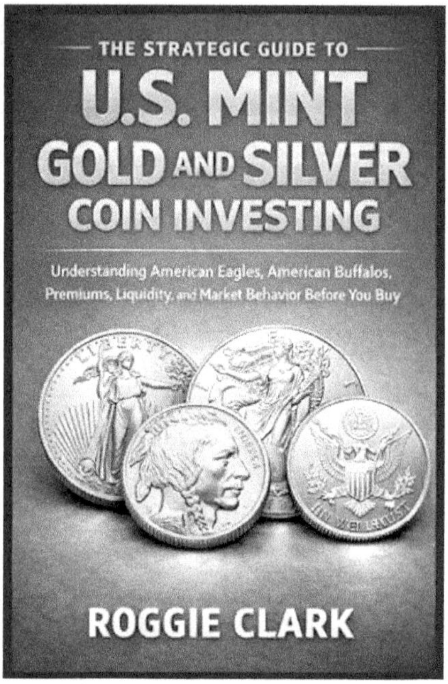

Rather than offering a general introduction to precious metals, this guide examines how American Gold Eagles, American Gold Buffalos, and Silver American Eagles behave in real investor markets.

https://www.amazon.com/Strategic-Guide-U-S-Silver-Investing/dp/B0GQKJF9K6

Copyright

Title: Macroeconomics and Microeconomics for Forex and Currency Traders
Author: Roggie Clark

Cover Design: Roggie Clark
Editing: Renee' Clark

Printed in the United States of America

Disclaimer

The views and opinions expressed in this publication are those of the author and do not necessarily reflect the official policies, positions, opinions, or viewpoints of any individual, company, organization, institution, agency, or entity referenced or mentioned within this work.

The author is not necessarily affiliated with, endorsed by, sponsored by, or compensated by any individuals, companies, organizations, brands, institutions, products, or services referenced within this publication unless specifically stated otherwise. Any examples, sample situations, stories, illustrations, or scenarios presented may be fictionalized or simplified for educational purposes. Any resemblance to actual persons, living or dead, businesses, or events is purely coincidental unless otherwise stated.

The information, ideas, strategies, concepts, techniques, opinions, suggestions, and educational materials contained in this publication are provided on an "as is" basis without warranties of any kind, either express or implied. While every effort has been made to provide accurate and current information, neither the author nor the publisher makes any representations or warranties regarding the completeness, accuracy, reliability, suitability, or applicability of the information presented.

This publication is intended solely for educational and informational purposes and should not be interpreted as professional advice of any kind, including but not limited to financial, investment, legal, tax, business, medical, mental health, educational, psychological, or other professional guidance. Readers should conduct their own independent research and consult appropriately qualified professionals before making decisions that may affect their finances, health, business, education, legal matters, personal circumstances, or other important areas of life.

Results, outcomes, and experiences may vary significantly among individuals. Neither the author nor the publisher guarantees any specific outcomes, results, earnings, performance improvements, personal achievements, or benefits resulting from the use of information contained in this publication.

By reading, accessing, or using this publication, you acknowledge and agree that the author and publisher shall not be held liable for any direct, indirect, incidental, consequential, financial, personal, emotional, or other damages, losses, or claims arising from the use, misuse, interpretation, or application of information contained within this publication. You assume full responsibility for any actions, decisions, and outcomes resulting from the use of this material.

Image Credits and Public Domain Notice

All images, illustrations, graphics, photographs, visual references, and related materials included in this publication are believed to be in the public domain, used under applicable licenses or permissions, created by the author or publisher, or obtained from sources that clearly identify them as available for lawful use.

The author and publisher have made a good faith effort to use only visual materials that are lawfully available for use and distribution. Where applicable, images and visual materials may have been resized, cropped, edited, enhanced, stylized, modified, reformatted, or arranged for educational, informational, design, formatting, or presentation purposes.

This publication is intended for educational, informational, and illustrative purposes only. The inclusion of any image, artwork, photograph, visual reference, symbol, historical material, design, or graphic element is not intended to claim ownership over public domain materials or any third-party intellectual property rights that remain with their respective owners.

If you believe any image or visual material included in this publication has been used in error, please contact the author or publisher so the matter may be reviewed and corrected in future editions or releases if necessary.

Any factual information, specifications, historical references, values, descriptions, statistics, or related content accompanying visual materials are provided for general informational purposes only and may change over time. Readers should conduct their own independent research and consult appropriate sources or qualified professionals when making decisions based on information presented in this publication.

This publication is independently produced and is not affiliated with, endorsed by, sponsored by, or associated with any company, organization, government agency, institution, trademark holder, or third party unless specifically stated otherwise.

Table of Contents

Introduction

Understanding the foreign exchange market requires more than knowing that one currency has risen while another has fallen. Behind those movements are economies, businesses, consumers, investors, financial institutions, governments, and central banks making decisions that can influence the demand for currencies around the world. Inflation changes purchasing power. Interest rates affect borrowing and investment. International trade creates demand for different currencies. Economic growth can attract capital, while uncertainty can encourage investors to move it elsewhere. For forex and currency traders, learning the economics behind these relationships provides a way to look beyond the price chart and begin understanding some of the forces that can influence exchange rates.

Why Economics Matters for Forex and Currency Traders

The **foreign exchange market**, commonly known as the forex or FX market, allows currencies to be exchanged with one another. It supports an enormous range of economic activity, from businesses paying international suppliers to investors purchasing assets in foreign countries.

Currency trading exists within this much larger system.

That distinction matters because it is easy for a beginner to encounter forex primarily through trading platforms. You see currency pairs, changing prices, charts, economic calendars, and buy and sell buttons. From that perspective, currencies can begin to look like numbers moving across a screen.

In reality, those currencies are connected to economies.

Consider a business in the United States purchasing products from a supplier in another country. Depending on how the transaction is structured, one currency may need to be exchanged for another before payment can occur. A multinational corporation may need to convert revenue earned overseas back into its domestic currency. An investor purchasing foreign assets may also need to exchange currencies.

Governments and central banks have their own reasons for participating in international currency markets, while traders and financial institutions may buy and sell currencies based on their expectations about future economic conditions.

Together, these activities create a market in which currencies are continuously being exchanged.

This is where economics becomes useful.

Macroeconomics examines the economy on a broad scale. It includes subjects such as inflation, economic growth, employment, interest rates, monetary policy, fiscal policy, and international trade.

These subjects are particularly relevant to currency traders because changing economic conditions can influence how market participants view a country's currency.

If inflation is increasing rapidly, for example, traders may begin thinking about how the country's central bank could respond. If economic growth is weakening, investors might reconsider their expectations for future interest rates. If international investment is flowing into a country, demand for its currency may be affected.

Microeconomics, on the other hand, focuses more closely on individual markets and the decisions made by consumers, businesses, and other participants.

For currency traders, concepts such as supply, demand, incentives, and market behavior provide another piece of the puzzle.

A business deciding to purchase products from another country may create a need for foreign currency. An investor deciding to purchase an overseas asset can create another currency transaction. Millions of individual decisions can collectively contribute to much larger movements of money between countries.

Macroeconomics helps us understand the broader environment in which those decisions occur. Microeconomics helps us understand some of the behaviors and market forces operating within that environment.

Forex traders can benefit from both perspectives.

Economics will not tell you with certainty what a currency will do next. Markets can respond unexpectedly, and currency prices are influenced by many variables at the same time. Instead, economics provides a framework for understanding why certain information matters and how different developments may be connected.

That framework is what we will build throughout this book.

What This Book Will Help You Understand

This book is designed to help you develop an economic foundation for understanding forex and currency markets without requiring an advanced economics background.

The goal is not to turn the reader into an economist.

The goal is to make economic information more useful.

Forex traders frequently encounter terms such as inflation, GDP, unemployment, interest rates, monetary policy, trade balances, consumer confidence, and economic growth. Knowing the definition of each term is helpful, but definitions alone do not provide much context.

The more useful question is:

What might this information mean for a currency?

That requires understanding relationships.

Suppose inflation begins rising faster than expected. Traders may start considering whether the central bank could respond by changing monetary policy. Expectations for interest rates may then change. Different interest-rate expectations can influence investment decisions and international capital flows, which may affect demand for currencies.

One economic development has now become connected to several others.

The same approach can be applied to economic growth.

Gross Domestic Product (GDP) is commonly used to measure the value of goods and services produced within an economy. A GDP report can provide information about whether economic activity is expanding or contracting.

But a currency trader should not stop at the number.

You might consider whether growth is accelerating or slowing, whether the result was stronger or weaker than expected, how it compares with conditions in another country, and what it could mean for future policy decisions.

Employment information can be examined similarly.

Strong employment conditions may indicate that businesses are hiring and economic activity is healthy. However, traders may also consider whether strong labor demand could contribute to wage pressures or inflation and how policymakers might respond.

This book will gradually connect these pieces.

You will learn how supply and demand can influence currency prices, how exchange rates express the relationship between two currencies, and why currencies must be analyzed comparatively rather than in isolation.

We will then examine inflation, purchasing power, interest rates, central banks, and monetary policy.

From there, we will explore important **economic indicators** and how they can contribute to fundamental analysis. Instead of simply memorizing what CPI, PCE, PPI, PMI, GDP, and employment reports measure, we will focus on why traders pay attention to them and how different indicators can help describe the condition of an economy.

International economics will also play an important role.

Currencies help facilitate economic activity across national borders. Imports, exports, international investment, capital flows, tariffs, and trade policies can therefore become relevant when examining exchange rates.

Finally, we will bring these concepts together by looking at economic cycles and comparing conditions between economies.

This last point is especially important.

Forex trading is inherently comparative.

If you are analyzing a currency pair, you are dealing with two currencies and, in many cases, two different economic environments.

Understanding one economy is only part of the job.

Looking Beyond Charts and Price Movements

Charts can provide valuable information about how a currency pair has behaved, but a chart does not contain the entire economic story.

Imagine that a currency suddenly begins strengthening.

Looking at the chart tells you that buyers have pushed the currency higher relative to another currency. It may show when the movement began, how large it has been, and how the current price compares with previous prices.

Economics encourages you to ask another question:

Why might demand have changed?

Perhaps an inflation report was different from what the market expected.

Perhaps a central bank changed its outlook for interest rates.

Perhaps economic growth surprised investors.

Perhaps international capital began moving toward the country.

Perhaps conditions in the other country deteriorated.

Or perhaps several developments occurred at the same time.

This approach is part of **fundamental analysis**, which examines underlying economic and financial conditions that may influence a market.

Fundamental analysis is not about finding a single economic indicator that predicts exchange rates.

Currency markets are rarely that simple.

Instead, traders can build an economic picture from multiple pieces of information.

Inflation may tell you something about price pressures.

Employment data may tell you something about the labor market.

GDP can provide information about economic growth.

Interest rates tell you something about borrowing conditions and monetary policy.

Trade data can provide information about the flow of goods and services between countries.

Central bank communications can provide clues about how policymakers view the economy and what they may do in the future.

Each piece adds context.

Expectations add another layer.

Markets often respond not only to whether economic information is positive or negative, but also to whether the information is different from what participants expected.

Suppose economists expect an economic indicator to show significant improvement. The report is eventually released and shows only modest improvement.

The economy technically improved.

However, the currency could still react negatively because the result was weaker than anticipated.

This is one reason economic analysis should not become a collection of rigid rules.

"Higher number equals stronger currency" is usually too simplistic.

"Lower number equals weaker currency" is usually too simplistic.

The better approach is to understand what the indicator measures, what the market expected, what the result suggests about the economy, and how it could influence future decisions by businesses, investors, consumers, governments, or central banks.

You also need to consider the other currency in the pair.

An economy can be performing poorly while its currency strengthens against the currency of an economy performing even worse. Likewise, an economy can be growing while its currency weakens because market participants expected stronger growth or because conditions elsewhere appear more attractive.

Currency values are relative.

Throughout this book, we will therefore focus less on memorizing isolated rules and more on understanding economic relationships. As those relationships become clearer, economic reports and currency movements can begin to look less like disconnected events and more like parts of a larger economic system.

Last Thoughts

Economics cannot remove uncertainty from forex trading, and understanding economic indicators does not guarantee that you will correctly predict currency movements. What economics can provide is context. It can help you understand why traders pay attention to inflation, why interest-rate expectations matter, why central bank decisions can influence markets, and why developments in international trade can affect currencies. Most importantly, it can help you begin looking beyond a price movement and asking what economic forces may be contributing to it. With that foundation established, we can begin with one of the most fundamental forces operating in any market: supply and demand.

Chapter 1: Supply, Demand, and How Currency Prices Move

Every exchange rate represents a market in which participants are willing to exchange one currency for another. Although forex charts can make currencies appear to move almost mechanically, the prices on those charts ultimately reflect decisions being made throughout the global economy. Businesses need currencies to conduct international commerce, investors move money between countries, financial institutions complete transactions for clients, governments and central banks participate in currency markets, and traders respond to changing economic expectations. Understanding these activities through supply and demand gives forex and currency traders a useful foundation for thinking about why exchange rates change.

Supply and Demand in the Foreign Exchange Market

We introduced supply and demand in the Introduction, but now we can examine how those forces operate specifically within the foreign exchange market.

Currencies are constantly being bought and sold for different reasons.

Consider an American company purchasing machinery from a European manufacturer. If the manufacturer requires payment in euros, the American company may need to exchange U.S. dollars for euros before completing the purchase.

From a simplified economic perspective, the company is supplying dollars while creating demand for euros.

Now imagine this happening across thousands of businesses and millions of transactions. Importers purchase foreign products. Exporters receive payments from customers overseas. Investors purchase assets in other countries. Companies move profits between international subsidiaries. Travelers exchange money before visiting another country.

Each transaction is relatively small when viewed against the entire global currency market, but together these activities contribute to the supply and demand for different currencies.

Investment can be particularly important.

Suppose international investors become increasingly interested in opportunities within a particular country. They may want to purchase government bonds, stocks, businesses, real estate, or other assets there.

Depending on the transaction, those investors may need the country's currency.

Greater investment activity can therefore contribute to increased currency demand.

The reverse is possible as well.

If investors become concerned about an economy and begin moving money elsewhere, they may sell assets denominated in that country's currency and exchange the proceeds for other currencies. These movements of money between countries are known as **capital flows**.

Capital flows help demonstrate why currencies are connected to much more than international trade.

Investment opportunities, economic growth, interest rates, political uncertainty, financial stability, and expectations about the future can all influence where investors decide to hold their money.

Changes in these decisions can change currency demand.

When demand for a currency increases relative to its supply, there can be upward pressure on its value relative to another currency. When supply increases relative to demand, there can be downward pressure.

When a currency becomes more valuable relative to another currency, this is known as **currency appreciation**.

When it becomes less valuable relative to another currency, this is known as **currency depreciation**.

Suppose international demand for products and investments from a particular country increases significantly. Foreign buyers may need more of that country's currency to complete their transactions. If other conditions remain the same, that additional demand could contribute to appreciation.

Now imagine investors suddenly become concerned about the country's economic outlook. Some may decide to move their capital elsewhere. That process could involve selling the domestic currency and purchasing foreign currencies, potentially contributing to depreciation.

These examples are intentionally simplified.

Real currency markets involve enormous numbers of participants acting for different reasons at the same time. Increased demand created by one group can be offset by increased selling from another. Economic developments can also affect several currencies simultaneously.

This is why supply and demand should not be treated as a formula that automatically predicts the next price movement.

Instead, it gives traders a framework for asking better questions.

Why might demand for this currency be increasing?

Why might investors be moving capital into or out of this economy?

What economic development could change those incentives?

Those questions will become increasingly useful as we introduce interest rates, inflation, economic indicators, trade, and central bank policy throughout the book.

Understanding Currency Pairs and Exchange Rates

Currencies have another characteristic that separates forex from many other markets.

A currency is priced relative to another currency.

A **currency pair** shows the relationship between two currencies in the foreign exchange market. EUR/USD, GBP/USD, USD/JPY, and USD/CAD are examples of currency pairs.

Each pair contains two sides.

The first currency is the **base currency**.

The second is the **quote currency**.

Consider EUR/USD.

EUR is the base currency, while USD is the quote currency.

Suppose EUR/USD has a hypothetical exchange rate of 1.10.

This means one euro is worth approximately 1.10 U.S. dollars at that exchange rate.

If EUR/USD increases from 1.10 to 1.15, the euro has appreciated relative to the dollar.

Another way of describing the same movement is that the dollar has depreciated relative to the euro.

This is an important way of thinking about forex because the same price movement tells us something about both currencies.

The relationship also means currency traders need to think comparatively.

Suppose the European economy is growing steadily.

That information alone does not tell us what EUR/USD should do.

What is happening in the United States?

Perhaps the European economy is growing at a healthy pace, but the U.S. economy is accelerating even faster. Investors may become increasingly interested in U.S. opportunities, potentially affecting demand for dollars.

Alternatively, U.S. growth could be weakening while European economic conditions improve.

The relative economic picture has changed again.

This is why describing a currency as simply "strong" or "weak" can sometimes be misleading.

Strong compared with which currency?

The U.S. dollar could appreciate against one currency while depreciating against another. Different countries can experience different combinations of growth, inflation, interest rates, trade conditions, and investor demand at the same time.

Exchange rates also have consequences outside financial markets.

Imagine a U.S. business that exports products to Europe.

Suppose one product costs $100.

If one dollar hypothetically exchanges for one euro, the $100 product would cost a European buyer approximately 100 euros before accounting for other expenses.

Now suppose the dollar strengthens considerably.

The same $100 product may require more euros to purchase. From the European customer's perspective, the American product has become more expensive even though the U.S. company never changed its dollar price.

That can influence demand.

A stronger domestic currency can make imported goods relatively more affordable because the currency can purchase more foreign currency. However, it can also make domestically produced exports more expensive for foreign customers.

A weaker currency can produce the opposite pressures.

Imports can become more expensive for domestic consumers and businesses, while exports may become more competitively priced for international customers.

These relationships show that exchange rates do not simply respond to economic conditions.

They can also influence economic conditions.

Currency movements can affect import costs, export competitiveness, business profits, consumer prices, and eventually inflation. Businesses operating internationally may therefore pay close attention to exchange rates even if they have no interest in speculative currency trading.

For forex traders, this relationship provides another reason to avoid looking at currencies in isolation.

A currency pair represents two currencies, two economic environments, and the constantly changing relationship between them.

Market Expectations, Sentiment, and Currency Demand

Supply and demand would be easier to interpret if market participants responded only to economic conditions that had already occurred.

Financial markets do not work that way.

Investors and traders constantly form opinions about what they believe may happen next.

Market expectations describe what participants collectively anticipate about future economic conditions, policies, or events.

Suppose a central bank has not changed interest rates, but investors increasingly believe that an interest-rate increase is coming.

Market participants do not necessarily have to wait for the central bank to act.

Some may begin changing their investments immediately based on what they expect the central bank to do in the future. Those decisions can affect demand for the currency before the anticipated policy change occurs.

This forward-looking behavior is an important part of understanding forex.

Economic reports provide a useful example.

Suppose economists expect a country's economy to grow by 2 percent, but a new report shows growth of 3 percent.

The result exceeded expectations.

Market participants may reconsider their assumptions about the strength of the economy, future inflation, or what the central bank might do next.

Now imagine the opposite.

Traders expect 4 percent growth, but the report shows 3 percent.

Three percent growth may still appear healthy when viewed by itself, but the result was weaker than anticipated.

The economic number is therefore only part of the information traders consider.

The relationship between the actual result and what the market expected can matter considerably.

The general expectation for an economic release is often called the **market consensus**.

When actual data differs substantially from the consensus, traders may need to quickly adjust their expectations.

Those adjustments can alter buying and selling decisions.

This helps explain why a seemingly positive economic report can sometimes be followed by a weakening currency, or why disappointing economic data can occasionally be followed by currency appreciation.

The market may have already expected something worse.

Expectations are also connected to **market sentiment**, which refers to the overall attitude or mood of market participants toward a market, economy, or financial environment.

Sentiment can shift between optimism and pessimism, confidence and uncertainty, or willingness and unwillingness to accept risk.

Imagine a period in which investors are confident about global economic growth.

They may become more willing to invest internationally, pursue new opportunities, and accept additional financial risk.

Now imagine a major event suddenly creates widespread uncertainty.

The same investors may become more concerned about preserving capital. They could reduce certain investments, move money between markets, or increase holdings they perceive as more stable.

Those decisions can change capital flows and currency demand.

Market expectations and sentiment are not always correct.

Traders can become overly optimistic. Investors can underestimate risks. Economic forecasts can be wrong. Unexpected events can completely change the outlook.

The important point is that expectations themselves can influence current behavior.

This leads to another phrase traders frequently encounter: **priced in**.

When information is described as priced in, it means market participants may have already adjusted their behavior based on an expected development, causing at least some of its anticipated effect to be reflected in current prices.

Suppose nearly everyone expects a central bank to increase interest rates at its next meeting.

By the time the announcement arrives, traders have had weeks to prepare.

If the bank does exactly what was expected, the currency may not react as dramatically as someone unfamiliar with market expectations might assume.

The more surprising information could instead come from what policymakers say about the future.

Will additional increases follow?

Are policymakers becoming more concerned about inflation?

Do they believe economic growth is weakening?

The answers can change expectations again.

This creates a continuous process.

Economic information affects expectations. Expectations influence the decisions of market participants. Those decisions alter supply and demand. Changes in supply and demand can influence exchange rates. New price movements and economic developments then affect expectations again.

For currency traders, understanding this process is more useful than assuming every economic development has a predetermined effect on a currency.

The market is not simply responding to what is happening.

It is also responding to what participants believe may happen next.

Last Thoughts

Supply and demand provide one of the most important foundations for understanding currency markets, but forex requires traders to think about those forces in a particular way. Currencies are exchanged for international trade, investment, business activity, financial transactions, and many other purposes, creating constantly changing demand across the global economy. Because currencies trade in pairs, those conditions must also be considered relative to another currency and another economy. Market expectations and sentiment add another layer because participants frequently make decisions based on what they believe will happen in the future rather than waiting for economic changes to occur. Understanding these relationships prepares us for the next major connection in currency economics: how inflation, interest rates, and central bank policy can influence the incentives and expectations of market participants.

Chapter 2: Inflation, Interest Rates, and Central Bank Policy

Inflation, interest rates, and central bank policy are some of the most closely connected economic forces in currency markets. Inflation affects the purchasing power of money, interest rates influence the cost of borrowing and the potential return available on certain investments, and central banks use monetary policy to influence economic conditions. Forex traders often pay close attention to all three because a change in one can alter expectations about the others. Understanding these relationships can help traders move beyond simply reacting to an economic announcement and begin considering what that announcement could mean for an economy and its currency.

Understanding Inflation and Purchasing Power

Inflation refers to a general increase in prices throughout an economy over time. When inflation occurs, the same amount of currency generally purchases fewer goods and services than it did previously.

This is where **purchasing power** becomes important.

Purchasing power describes how much a particular amount of money can buy.

Imagine that $100 allows you to purchase a particular combination of groceries, transportation, and other everyday necessities. Several years later, the same combination costs $110. Even though the number printed on your money has not changed, its purchasing power has declined.

For consumers, this can mean higher living expenses.

For businesses, inflation can mean higher costs for materials, labor, transportation, energy, and other inputs.

For investors and currency traders, inflation can provide information about what is happening within an economy and what policymakers might do in response.

Not all inflation develops for exactly the same reason.

Demand-pull inflation can occur when overall demand for goods and services grows faster than an economy's ability to supply them. Consumers and businesses compete for available products and services, placing upward pressure on prices.

Suppose an economy is growing rapidly. Employment is strong, household incomes are rising, businesses are expanding, and consumers are spending more.

If production cannot increase quickly enough to meet that additional demand, prices may begin rising.

Cost-push inflation develops from another direction.

Instead of demand increasing, businesses experience higher production costs. Energy prices might increase, raw materials may become more expensive, transportation costs could rise, or businesses may have to pay higher wages.

Companies then have several choices.

They can absorb some of the additional cost and accept smaller profit margins. They can attempt to become more efficient. Or they can pass some of those costs to customers through higher prices.

If similar cost increases occur throughout an economy, they can contribute to broader inflation.

Another concept is **built-in inflation**, which can occur when previous price increases begin influencing future wages and prices.

Workers who experience higher living costs may seek higher wages. Businesses facing higher wage expenses may then increase prices. Those price increases can contribute to additional demands for higher wages.

These different forms of inflation matter because traders should not assume that every increase in prices tells the same economic story.

Consider two countries.

Country A is experiencing rising inflation because consumer demand is exceptionally strong and the economy is expanding quickly.

Country B is experiencing similar inflation because a major supply disruption has increased production costs while its economy is barely growing.

The inflation rate may look similar, but the economic environments are very different.

Country B could even face **stagflation**, a difficult condition in which high inflation exists alongside weak or stagnant economic growth and elevated unemployment.

For policymakers, this creates a challenge.

Actions designed to slow inflation can also reduce economic activity. Actions designed to stimulate a weak economy can sometimes add to inflationary pressure.

Currency traders therefore need to consider inflation within the broader economic environment.

Inflation can also affect currencies through international purchasing power.

If prices in one country consistently increase much faster than prices elsewhere, the relative purchasing power of its currency can change over time. Businesses and consumers may alter what they import or export, while investors may reconsider the real return they are receiving after accounting for inflation.

However, one of the most important mistakes to avoid is assuming:

Higher inflation automatically means a weaker currency.

The relationship is more complicated.

Higher inflation might create concerns about purchasing power, but it could also increase expectations that a central bank will raise interest rates. Those changing interest-rate expectations may influence investor demand for the currency.

This is why forex traders often respond not only to inflation itself, but also to what inflation could mean for monetary policy.

To understand that connection, we need to look more closely at interest rates.

How Interest Rates Can Influence Currency Values

Interest rates affect nearly every part of an economy.

Consumers encounter them when borrowing money for homes, automobiles, education, or other purchases. Businesses consider them when financing equipment, expansion, inventory, and other investments. Investors consider them when deciding where to place their capital.

For forex traders, that last relationship is particularly important.

Imagine an investor deciding between comparable interest-bearing assets in two different countries.

One offers a relatively low return.

The other offers a substantially higher return.

If the investor believes the additional return justifies the risks involved, the higher-rate country may become more attractive.

Purchasing assets there may require obtaining that country's currency.

This creates a connection between interest rates, international investment, capital flows, and currency demand.

A particularly useful concept is the **interest rate differential**, which is the difference between the interest rates associated with two economies.

Because currencies trade in pairs, traders are often interested in these differences rather than examining one country's interest rate alone.

Suppose Country A has an interest rate of 5 percent while Country B has a rate of 2 percent.

There is a three-percentage-point differential between them.

Now imagine Country A begins lowering rates while Country B leaves its rates unchanged.

The difference between the two countries is narrowing.

Even though Country A may still have the higher rate, the relative advantage has changed.

That change can affect investor expectations.

The direction of monetary policy can therefore matter alongside the current interest rate.

A country with a 4 percent rate that is expected to raise rates further can present a different economic situation from a country with a 4 percent rate that is expected to begin cutting rates.

Forex markets can respond to where participants believe rates are going.

This returns us to the role of expectations introduced in Chapter 1.

Investors do not necessarily wait until an interest-rate decision occurs before reacting.

If economic information strongly suggests that rates may rise in the future, traders and investors may begin adjusting their positions beforehand. If the expected increase eventually occurs, some of the market reaction may already have taken place.

Interest rates also influence currencies through their effects on the broader economy.

Higher rates generally make borrowing more expensive.

A business considering a loan for a new facility may decide that the project is no longer attractive at the higher borrowing cost. A household might postpone purchasing a home or vehicle. Consumers carrying variable-rate debt may have less disposable income available for other purchases.

As borrowing and spending slow, economic activity can cool.

Lower interest rates can work in the opposite direction by reducing borrowing costs and potentially encouraging spending and investment.

This creates an important balancing act.

A central bank may want rates high enough to control excessive inflation but not so high that economic activity slows more than intended.

For currency traders, the question is therefore not simply whether high rates are "good" for a currency or low rates are "bad."

Higher rates may attract capital, but extremely restrictive rates can eventually weaken economic activity.

Lower rates may reduce the return available on some assets, but they may also support borrowing, investment, and economic recovery.

The broader environment matters.

Risk matters as well.

A country could offer extremely high interest rates because investors perceive substantial inflation, political instability, or financial risk. The potential return may be higher, but investors might still avoid the currency if they believe the risk of holding it is too great.

This is another reason simple rules can become misleading.

Interest rates influence incentives, but they do not operate alone.

Inflation, growth, stability, expectations, and monetary policy all contribute to the economic picture.

Central Banks, Monetary Policy, and Currency Markets

A **central bank** is an institution responsible for managing important aspects of a country's or currency area's monetary system.

Different central banks operate under different mandates and institutional structures, but their responsibilities can include maintaining price stability, influencing interest rates, supporting financial stability, managing currency reserves, and helping guide monetary conditions within the economy.

The actions central banks take to influence money, credit, and economic conditions are broadly described as monetary policy.

One of the most recognizable monetary policy tools is the policy interest rate.

When inflation becomes persistently high, a central bank may decide to **tighten monetary policy**.

Monetary tightening generally refers to policies intended to make financial conditions more restrictive. Raising interest rates is one way a central bank can do this.

Higher borrowing costs can discourage some spending and investment.

If demand throughout the economy slows, pressure on prices may eventually decrease.

The process is not immediate.

A rate increase today does not necessarily cause inflation to fall tomorrow. Monetary policy can take time to work through lending, business investment, housing, employment, consumer spending, and other parts of the economy.

Central banks must therefore make decisions partly based on where they believe the economy is heading.

When economic conditions are weak, policymakers may instead **ease monetary policy**.

Lowering interest rates is one form of monetary easing. Cheaper borrowing can encourage households and businesses to spend and invest, potentially supporting economic activity.

Central banks can also use additional policy tools depending on economic circumstances and the structure of the country's financial system.

For forex traders, the important point is that monetary policy can alter economic incentives.

Suppose one central bank is tightening monetary policy because inflation remains elevated while another is easing policy because economic growth is weak.

Investors comparing the two economies now face very different interest-rate environments.

Those differences can influence capital flows and currency demand.

However, currency markets do not pay attention only to what central banks do.

They also pay close attention to what policymakers say.

Central banks regularly communicate their assessments of inflation, employment, growth, financial conditions, and potential future policy.

A central bank that appears increasingly concerned about inflation may create expectations of tighter future policy.

A central bank that appears increasingly concerned about weak economic growth may create expectations of easier policy.

Traders sometimes describe these general policy attitudes using the terms **hawkish** and **dovish**.

A hawkish policy stance generally emphasizes controlling inflation and may be associated with maintaining higher interest rates or tightening monetary conditions.

A dovish stance generally places greater emphasis on supporting economic activity and may be associated with lower rates or easier monetary conditions.

These terms should not be treated as permanent labels.

A central bank can become more hawkish or more dovish as economic conditions change.

Imagine inflation has been falling for several months.

A central bank that previously emphasized the need for high rates may begin acknowledging that price pressures are easing. Even if policymakers leave the interest rate unchanged at the current meeting, traders might interpret the change in language as a signal that rate cuts could become more likely in the future.

The currency market may respond to the changing expectation rather than waiting for the first actual rate cut.

This is why central bank announcements can sometimes create significant currency movements even when the policy rate itself does not change.

The new information may be in the outlook.

Forex traders can therefore think about central bank policy in three layers.

What is the central bank doing now?

What does the central bank appear likely to do next?

And how does that compare with what the market already expects?

That final question is critical.

If traders overwhelmingly expect an interest-rate increase and the central bank delivers exactly that increase, the decision itself may contain relatively little new information.

But if policymakers unexpectedly indicate that additional increases are unlikely, expectations can change quickly.

This interaction between inflation, interest rates, central bank communication, and expectations is one of the clearest examples of why economic concepts need to be studied together rather than separately.

Inflation can influence monetary policy.

Monetary policy can influence interest rates.

Interest rates can influence borrowing and investment.

Investment decisions can affect capital flows.

Capital flows can influence currency demand.

And throughout the process, traders are continuously forming expectations about what may happen next.

Understanding that chain is far more useful than memorizing that one particular central bank action must always cause a currency to move in one particular direction.

Last Thoughts

Inflation, interest rates, and central bank policy form an important relationship within forex and currency markets. Inflation can reduce purchasing power and influence expectations about future monetary policy, while interest rates can change borrowing conditions, investment incentives, and international capital flows. Central banks attempt to balance these forces as economic conditions evolve, and currency markets often respond not only to their current decisions but also to expectations about what they may do next. For traders, the goal is not to memorize simple rules such as "higher rates equal a stronger currency." It is to understand the economic chain connecting inflation, policy, investment, expectations, and currency demand. In the next chapter, we will look at the economic indicators traders use to gather the information needed to evaluate those changing conditions.

Chapter 3: Economic Indicators and Fundamental Analysis

Economic indicators give forex and currency traders a way to evaluate what is happening inside an economy. Instead of relying only on price movements or general impressions, traders can examine information about economic growth, employment, inflation, business activity, and consumer confidence. These reports become particularly useful when they are considered together rather than treated as isolated numbers. Fundamental analysis involves interpreting this broader economic picture, comparing it with expectations, and considering how changing conditions could influence central bank policy, investment decisions, and ultimately currency demand.

GDP, Employment, and Economic Growth

Gross Domestic Product, or GDP, was introduced earlier as a measure of the value of goods and services produced within an economy.

For currency traders, GDP can provide a broad indication of whether economic activity is growing or contracting.

An economy with increasing production, business activity, investment, and consumer spending may experience rising GDP. An economy experiencing declining activity may see GDP growth slow or turn negative.

However, simply knowing whether GDP increased is not enough.

Traders can consider the rate of growth, how that growth compares with previous periods, whether the result met expectations, and how the economy compares with another country.

Suppose one economy grows by 2 percent.

Viewed alone, that number does not tell us very much.

If the economy previously grew by 1 percent, the new result could indicate accelerating activity. If it previously grew by 4 percent, the same 2 percent result could indicate substantial slowing.

Expectations add another layer.

If economists expected 1.5 percent growth and the economy grew by 2 percent, the result exceeded expectations.

If economists expected 3 percent growth, the same 2 percent result would be disappointing relative to the market consensus.

This is why traders need context.

Another distinction worth understanding is **nominal GDP** compared with **real GDP**.

Nominal GDP measures economic output using current prices. This means an increase in prices can contribute to a higher nominal GDP figure even if the actual quantity of goods and services being produced has not increased by the same amount.

Real GDP adjusts for changes in prices, making it useful when attempting to understand changes in actual economic output.

Economic growth also connects to many of the concepts we have already discussed.

A rapidly growing economy may create additional demand for workers. Strong employment can support household income and consumer spending. Increasing demand can encourage businesses to expand production.

However, an economy that grows too quickly can also experience greater inflationary pressure.

If demand begins exceeding the economy's ability to supply goods and services, prices may rise more rapidly. That can affect expectations about central bank policy and interest rates.

Weak economic growth creates different concerns.

Businesses experiencing declining demand may postpone investments, reduce production, or slow hiring. Consumers worried about economic conditions may become more cautious about spending.

This is where employment indicators become particularly valuable.

The **unemployment rate** measures the percentage of people within the labor force who are unemployed and actively seeking work.

A declining unemployment rate can indicate improving labor-market conditions, while a rising unemployment rate can suggest weakening employment.

However, unemployment data also requires context.

A lower unemployment rate does not necessarily mean every aspect of the labor market is improving.

One reason is the **labor force participation rate**, which measures the proportion of the working-age population that is employed or actively seeking employment.

Imagine that the unemployment rate falls partly because some unemployed individuals stop looking for work.

Those individuals may no longer be counted as unemployed under the standard definition because they have left the labor force.

Looking at participation alongside unemployment can therefore provide a more complete picture.

Job creation can also matter.

If businesses are consistently adding workers, traders may interpret that as evidence of healthy economic activity. Strong demand for labor can also influence wages.

Wages connect employment to inflation.

When workers earn more, households may have greater capacity to spend. Higher labor costs can also increase expenses for businesses. Depending on the broader environment, strong wage growth can contribute to inflationary pressure.

That means an employment report can potentially affect expectations about monetary policy.

Suppose employment growth is stronger than expected, unemployment remains low, and wages are increasing quickly.

Traders may begin asking whether the labor market is strong enough to keep inflation elevated.

If they believe it is, expectations about future interest rates could change.

Now consider the opposite situation.

Job creation is slowing, unemployment is increasing, and economic growth is weakening.

Traders might begin expecting the central bank to place greater emphasis on supporting the economy, potentially increasing expectations for easier monetary policy.

GDP and employment data therefore help traders answer a broader question:

Is the economy strengthening, weakening, or somewhere in between?

The answer becomes more useful when combined with information about prices.

CPI, PCE, PPI, and Measuring Inflation

Inflation is not observed through a single universal measurement.

Economists and policymakers use different indicators to examine price changes throughout an economy. Three measures forex traders may frequently encounter are the **Consumer Price Index (CPI)**, **Personal Consumption Expenditures Price Index (PCE)**, and **Producer Price Index (PPI)**.

Each provides a different perspective.

CPI measures changes in the prices consumers pay for a collection of goods and services.

Because it focuses on consumer prices, CPI is frequently used as a broad measure of changes in the cost of living.

Imagine that the prices of housing, transportation, food, clothing, and other consumer expenses are increasing.

CPI attempts to capture changes across a broader collection of those expenses rather than focusing on the price of a single item.

Traders commonly look at both headline and underlying measures of inflation.

Headline inflation generally includes the full collection of items measured by a particular inflation index.

Core inflation removes certain categories that can experience particularly large short-term price fluctuations, commonly food and energy.

Why remove anything?

Suppose energy prices temporarily surge because of an unexpected disruption.

Headline inflation could increase substantially even though price pressures elsewhere in the economy remain relatively stable.

A core measure can help policymakers and market participants examine whether inflation appears to be spreading more broadly.

That does not make food or energy unimportant.

Consumers still have to purchase them.

The different measures simply answer somewhat different questions.

PCE provides another perspective on consumer prices.

Like CPI, it tracks changes in prices paid for goods and services, but its construction and weighting differ. It can account differently for changes in consumer spending patterns as households substitute between products.

Forex traders do not necessarily need to become experts in the statistical methodology behind every inflation index.

What matters is understanding that policymakers may place greater emphasis on particular measures when evaluating price stability.

In the United States, for example, PCE receives considerable attention in discussions of monetary policy.

Traders may also encounter **Core PCE**, which attempts to provide a view of underlying price pressures by excluding volatile food and energy categories.

PPI approaches inflation from another part of the economy.

Rather than concentrating primarily on the prices consumers pay, PPI measures changes in prices received by producers.

This can provide information about price pressures occurring earlier in the production process.

Imagine a manufacturer facing higher costs throughout its supply chain.

The company may absorb those increases.

It may become more efficient.

Or it may eventually raise the prices charged to customers.

This is why producer prices can sometimes provide useful information about potential inflationary pressures.

However, traders should avoid assuming that rising PPI automatically means consumer inflation will rise by the same amount.

Businesses do not always pass every cost increase directly to customers. Competition, consumer demand, existing contracts, productivity improvements, and profit margins can all influence what happens next.

The more useful approach is to consider several inflation indicators together.

Is consumer inflation accelerating?

Are underlying price pressures persistent?

Are producer prices increasing?

Are wages rising?

Is demand throughout the economy strong?

How is the central bank interpreting these developments?

These questions turn inflation data into economic analysis.

Expectations remain important as well.

Suppose CPI inflation falls from 4 percent to 3.5 percent.

At first glance, that appears to be encouraging evidence that inflation is slowing.

But suppose the market expected inflation to fall to 3 percent.

The actual result is lower than the previous reading but higher than expected.

Traders may interpret the report as evidence that inflation is proving more persistent than anticipated.

That could influence expectations for interest rates.

Another report could create the opposite situation.

Inflation might still be relatively high, but if it falls substantially faster than expected, traders could begin anticipating that the central bank will have greater flexibility to ease monetary policy in the future.

This is why the direction of inflation, the level of inflation, and the difference between actual and expected inflation can all matter.

No single number tells the entire story.

PMI, Consumer Confidence, and Reading Economic Conditions

Some economic indicators help traders evaluate conditions before they are fully reflected in broader measures such as GDP.

One commonly followed example is the **Purchasing Managers' Index (PMI)**.

PMI surveys purchasing managers and businesses to gather information about current conditions in areas such as production, new orders, employment, inventories, and business activity.

Because businesses make purchasing and production decisions in response to changing demand, PMI can provide relatively timely information about whether activity appears to be expanding or contracting.

PMI readings are commonly interpreted around a level of 50.

A reading above 50 generally indicates expansion in the activity being measured, while a reading below 50 generally indicates contraction.

But again, context matters.

Suppose PMI is 52.

That suggests expansion.

However, if the previous reading was 58, business activity may still be expanding while losing momentum.

Now suppose PMI rises from 47 to 49.

The reading remains below 50, indicating contraction, but conditions may be deteriorating less rapidly.

Direction and momentum can therefore matter alongside the headline number.

Different PMI reports can also focus on different portions of an economy, such as manufacturing or services.

This distinction can be particularly important when comparing countries.

Manufacturing may represent a larger share of economic activity in one country, while services dominate another. Traders should therefore consider the structure of the economy rather than assuming every indicator has identical importance everywhere.

Another useful measure is the **Consumer Confidence Index (CCI)**.

Consumer confidence attempts to measure how optimistic or pessimistic consumers feel about economic conditions.

Why should currency traders care about how consumers feel?

Consumer behavior is an important part of economic activity.

When households feel confident about their employment prospects and financial circumstances, they may be more willing to make purchases, take on certain financial commitments, or spend discretionary income.

When confidence deteriorates, consumers may become more cautious.

They might postpone major purchases, increase savings, or reduce discretionary spending.

If enough households change their behavior, the effects can appear throughout the economy.

Businesses may experience weaker sales.

Production may slow.

Hiring plans may change.

Economic growth may weaken.

Consumer confidence can therefore provide another clue about the direction of economic activity.

Like other indicators, confidence data should not be interpreted alone.

Consumers can report pessimistic attitudes while continuing to spend. Confidence can improve without immediately producing stronger economic growth.

The indicator is one piece of evidence.

Forex traders can use PMI, consumer confidence, GDP, employment, and inflation data to gradually build a broader picture.

Suppose manufacturing and services PMIs are improving.

Consumer confidence is rising.

Employment remains strong.

GDP growth is accelerating.

Taken together, those indicators might suggest an economy gaining momentum.

Now add inflation.

If inflation is relatively stable, policymakers may be comfortable with the growth.

If inflation is already significantly above the desired level and beginning to accelerate again, the same economic strength could create concerns about additional price pressure.

The interpretation changes.

This is the essence of fundamental analysis.

You are not searching for one magical economic report that tells you whether to buy or sell a currency.

You are attempting to understand the economic environment.

Forex traders can make this process more manageable by asking a few consistent questions whenever new data becomes available.

What does the indicator measure?

Is the result improving or deteriorating?

How does it compare with expectations?

How does it fit with other recent economic information?

Could it change expectations about central bank policy?

And how do these conditions compare with the economy behind the other currency in the pair?

That final comparison is especially important.

Suppose both economies represented by a currency pair are growing.

If one is accelerating while the other is slowing, their economic directions are becoming increasingly different.

Suppose inflation is falling in both.

If one central bank is nevertheless expected to maintain high rates while the other is expected to begin cutting rates, their monetary policy outlooks may still diverge.

Individual indicators become more meaningful when placed within these relationships.

This is also why traders should be cautious about reacting emotionally to a single economic release.

One report can be surprising.

One report can temporarily change expectations.

But economies are complex systems, and trends usually become clearer when multiple pieces of information begin pointing in a similar direction.

Economic indicators are therefore best thought of as signals contributing to a larger picture rather than instructions telling traders exactly what to do.

The better you understand what those signals measure, the easier it becomes to interpret economic news within the context of currency markets.

Last Thoughts

Economic indicators help forex and currency traders replace vague assumptions about an economy with measurable information about growth, employment, inflation, business activity, and consumer conditions. GDP and employment reports can provide insight into economic strength, CPI, PCE, and PPI can reveal different aspects of inflation, while PMI and consumer confidence can offer additional clues about the direction of economic activity. The greatest value comes from connecting these indicators rather than interpreting them individually. A strong employment report means something different when inflation is high than when inflation is falling, just as improving GDP can have different implications depending on what the market expected. Fundamental analysis is ultimately about building that larger economic picture and then comparing it with the conditions surrounding another currency. In the next chapter, we will expand that picture beyond individual economies by examining global trade and international currency flows.

Chapter 4: Global Trade and International Currency Flows

Currencies play an essential role in connecting economies. Businesses import products and materials, exporters sell goods and services to customers abroad, investors purchase foreign assets, and governments establish policies that influence how easily money and products move across borders. Many of these activities eventually involve exchanging one currency for another. For forex and currency traders, international trade provides another way to understand where currency demand can come from, while international investment reveals how quickly capital can move between economies. Trade policies can alter these relationships further by changing costs, incentives, and expectations throughout global markets.

Balance of Trade, Imports, Exports, and Currency Demand

Countries continuously buy and sell goods and services across international borders.

An **import** is a good or service purchased from another country.

An **export** is a good or service sold to another country.

These transactions can create demand for currencies because buyers and sellers operating in different countries may use different forms of money.

Imagine an American retailer purchasing products from a manufacturer located in Europe. If the European manufacturer requires payment in euros, the American business may need to exchange dollars for euros.

The commercial transaction has therefore created a currency transaction.

Now consider the opposite situation.

A European company purchases equipment from an American manufacturer and needs U.S. dollars to complete the transaction. That purchase could create demand for dollars.

Individual transactions like these occur constantly throughout the global economy.

When economists examine a country's exports relative to its imports, one measure they may use is the **balance of trade**.

A country has a **trade surplus** when the value of its exports exceeds the value of its imports over a particular period.

A **trade deficit** occurs when imports exceed exports.

At first glance, it might seem reasonable to assume that a trade surplus must strengthen a currency while a trade deficit must weaken it.

The relationship is not always that simple.

A country running a trade surplus may experience substantial foreign demand for its goods and services, potentially creating demand for its currency. However, the actual currency effect depends on how transactions are settled, where businesses hold their earnings, investment flows, monetary policy, and many other factors.

Likewise, a country can maintain a trade deficit for extended periods while still attracting enormous amounts of international investment.

This is why trade data should be treated as part of the larger economic picture rather than a standalone predictor of exchange rates.

Currency values can also influence trade.

Suppose a country's currency appreciates significantly.

Foreign products may become relatively less expensive for domestic consumers because their stronger currency can purchase more foreign currency. This may make imports more attractive.

Exporters can face a different situation.

Their products may become more expensive when priced in the currencies of foreign customers.

Imagine a U.S. manufacturer sells a piece of equipment for $10,000.

If the dollar appreciates considerably against the currency used by a foreign customer, that customer may need substantially more of their local currency to purchase the same $10,000 product.

The American manufacturer has not changed its price.

The exchange rate changed the price from the foreign customer's perspective.

That can influence international demand.

Currency depreciation can create the opposite pressures.

Imported products and materials can become more expensive because domestic buyers need more of their currency to purchase the necessary foreign currency.

Meanwhile, exports may become relatively less expensive for foreign customers.

This is one reason policymakers and businesses pay attention to exchange rates even when they are not involved in currency trading.

Currency movements can influence business competitiveness.

They can change production costs.

They can affect consumer prices.

They can influence corporate earnings.

They can even contribute to inflation when a weaker currency makes imported energy, materials, food, equipment, or other products more expensive.

This phenomenon is sometimes described as **imported inflation**.

Suppose a country depends heavily on imported fuel.

If its currency depreciates substantially against the currency used to price that fuel, domestic buyers may have to spend more simply because of the exchange-rate change.

Transportation and production costs could then increase throughout the economy.

International trade therefore creates a two-way relationship.

Trade can influence demand for currencies, while currency values can influence the cost and competitiveness of international trade.

For forex traders, understanding that relationship provides useful context when interpreting trade data and longer-term currency movements.

International Investment and Capital Flows

International trade is not the only reason currencies move between countries.

Investment can generate enormous currency flows as well.

Businesses build factories abroad. Investment funds purchase foreign stocks and bonds. Companies acquire businesses in other countries. Individuals purchase overseas property. Governments and institutions hold financial assets denominated in multiple currencies.

These activities can create international capital flows.

One useful distinction is between **foreign direct investment (FDI)** and **portfolio investment**.

Foreign direct investment generally involves making a substantial, longer-term investment in business operations or assets located in another country.

Suppose a manufacturer headquartered in one country decides to build a production facility in another.

The company may purchase land, construct buildings, hire workers, purchase equipment, and establish local operations.

Depending on how the investment is structured, significant amounts of capital may need to be converted into the local currency.

Portfolio investment is different.

Instead of establishing or controlling a business operation, investors purchase financial assets such as stocks or bonds.

A global investment fund, for example, might decide that government bonds in another country offer an attractive combination of return and risk.

Purchasing those bonds may create demand for that country's currency.

This brings us back to interest rates.

If interest rates in one economy become more attractive relative to those available elsewhere, some international investors may move capital toward that economy.

However, investors rarely consider yield alone.

They may also evaluate inflation, economic growth, political stability, government finances, financial-market liquidity, and currency risk.

A high interest rate may appear attractive until the investor believes the currency could depreciate enough to eliminate the additional return.

Imagine an investor converts $100,000 into another currency to purchase foreign bonds.

The investment earns a strong return.

But when the investor eventually sells the bonds and converts the proceeds back into dollars, the foreign currency has depreciated substantially.

Some or even all of the investment return could be lost during the currency conversion.

This is **exchange-rate risk**, which is the possibility that changes in currency values will affect the value of an international transaction or investment.

Businesses face similar risks.

Suppose an American company earns significant revenue in another country. When those foreign earnings are converted into dollars, the exchange rate affects how much the company ultimately receives.

A favorable currency movement could increase the dollar value of those earnings.

An unfavorable movement could reduce it.

Businesses and investors sometimes attempt to manage this uncertainty through **currency hedging**.

Hedging generally involves taking financial steps intended to reduce exposure to unfavorable currency movements.

The purpose is not necessarily to profit from predicting exchange rates.

A business may simply want greater certainty.

Imagine that a company knows it must pay a foreign supplier three months from now. If the exchange rate changes substantially before payment is due, the company's cost could unexpectedly increase.

A hedging arrangement may allow the business to reduce some of that uncertainty.

This illustrates an important distinction between participants in the foreign exchange market.

Not everyone exchanging currencies is attempting to speculate on their future value.

Some participants need currencies because they are conducting business.

Others are investing internationally.

Some are managing existing currency risks.

Others are trading based on their expectations about future movements.

All of these motivations contribute to currency supply and demand.

Capital flows can also change much faster than physical trade.

Building a factory in another country takes considerable time. Shipping products internationally also involves production, transportation, and logistics.

Financial capital can sometimes move across borders almost immediately.

If investors suddenly change their outlook for an economy, large amounts of money can potentially be repositioned quickly.

That makes expectations particularly important.

A change in anticipated interest rates, political uncertainty, financial instability, or economic growth can alter the attractiveness of an economy before the underlying economic data changes significantly.

Forex traders should therefore think about capital flows as another link between economics and currency demand.

The question is not simply whether an economy is performing well.

It is whether international investors find that economy relatively attractive compared with the alternatives available elsewhere.

Tariffs, Trade Policy, and Exchange Rates

International trade does not occur without rules.

Governments establish taxes, regulations, trade agreements, restrictions, and other policies that influence how goods and services move across borders.

One of the most familiar trade policies is a **tariff**, which is a tax or duty imposed on imported goods.

Governments may use tariffs for several reasons.

A country might want to protect a domestic industry from foreign competition. Policymakers might use tariffs as part of a trade negotiation. Governments may also argue that certain industries require protection for strategic or national-security reasons.

Whatever the motivation, tariffs change economic incentives.

Suppose imported steel becomes subject to a new tariff.

Domestic steel producers may benefit because foreign steel becomes more expensive.

Businesses that use imported steel as an input face a different situation.

Their production costs may increase.

Some businesses may absorb the additional expense, while others may increase prices, find alternative suppliers, or shift production.

Consumers can eventually encounter some of these changes as well.

For currency traders, the important point is that trade policy can affect several economic relationships at once.

Tariffs can alter import demand.

They can affect business costs.

They can contribute to changes in consumer prices.

They can influence economic growth.

They can encourage businesses to relocate supply chains.

And they can trigger responses from other governments.

A **retaliatory tariff** occurs when another country responds to a tariff by imposing additional trade restrictions of its own.

This can escalate into a broader trade dispute.

Imagine Country A places tariffs on products from Country B.

Country B responds with tariffs on products from Country A.

Exporters in both countries may face weaker demand or higher barriers. Businesses dependent on imported materials may experience rising costs. Investors may become uncertain about future growth.

Currency markets may then respond to the expected economic consequences.

But once again, there is no universal rule stating that tariffs must cause a currency to strengthen or weaken.

Suppose traders believe a tariff will significantly damage one country's export sector.

Its currency might come under pressure.

But suppose the same policy is expected to reduce imports and improve certain domestic industries.

Some market participants could interpret the economic consequences differently.

The other country's response matters too.

This is why trade-policy analysis requires context.

Free trade agreements attempt to reduce or eliminate certain barriers to commerce between participating countries.

Reducing tariffs can make it easier or less expensive for businesses to purchase products internationally, potentially increasing trade between participating economies.

However, trade agreements can also create winners and losers.

Businesses that gain access to new customers may benefit, while companies suddenly facing lower-cost foreign competition may struggle.

Supply chains can move between countries.

Employment patterns can change.

Investment can follow those changes.

Forex traders do not need to determine whether every trade policy is economically "good" or "bad."

The more useful objective is understanding how the policy changes incentives.

Will businesses import more or less?

Could exporters gain or lose access to an important market?

Might production costs rise?

Could inflation be affected?

Will companies move production?

Could international investment patterns change?

How might the policy affect economic growth?

And perhaps most importantly, are the consequences different for the two economies represented by the currency pair?

Trade policy can also influence market expectations before a policy actually takes effect.

If governments announce negotiations over major tariffs, investors may begin estimating the potential consequences immediately.

Businesses may postpone investments.

Importers might increase orders before tariffs take effect.

Companies may begin searching for alternative suppliers.

Traders may adjust their currency expectations.

The economic response can therefore begin before the official policy change.

This reinforces a theme that runs throughout currency analysis.

Forex markets are forward-looking.

Market participants are continuously attempting to estimate how today's developments could change tomorrow's economic conditions.

International trade and trade policy add another set of information to that process.

Last Thoughts

Global trade and international investment help explain why currencies are constantly being exchanged far beyond the activities of individual forex traders. Imports and exports can create demand for foreign currencies, while changing exchange rates can influence the price and competitiveness of internationally traded goods. Investment adds another major source of currency flows as businesses and investors move capital between countries in search of opportunities, returns, stability, or diversification. Trade policies such as tariffs can change these incentives further by affecting costs, supply chains, inflation, growth, and expectations. For currency traders, the important lesson is that international economic relationships are interconnected. Money moves between countries because goods, services, investments, and financial obligations move between them as well. In the next chapter, we will examine how these relationships can change as economies move through different stages of the economic cycle.

Chapter 5: Economic Cycles and Changing Currency Markets

Economies rarely grow at the same pace forever. Periods of stronger production, employment, investment, and consumer activity can eventually give way to slower growth, while periods of economic weakness can eventually transition into recovery. These changes are commonly described through economic cycles. For forex and currency traders, understanding these cycles can provide important context because inflation, interest rates, central bank policy, investment flows, and market expectations can all change as an economy moves from one stage to another. The challenge is that countries do not necessarily move through these stages at the same time, making the relative position of two economies especially important when analyzing a currency pair.

Expansion, Peaks, Contractions, and Troughs

An **economic cycle** describes the recurring periods of growth and decline that occur within an economy over time.

Although every cycle develops differently, it is commonly described using four broad stages: expansion, peak, contraction, and trough.

An **expansion** is a period during which economic activity is generally increasing.

Businesses may experience stronger demand.

Production can increase.

Companies may hire additional employees.

Consumer spending may rise.

Investment may increase as businesses become more confident about future opportunities.

GDP growth may strengthen as these activities spread throughout the economy.

For currency traders, expansion can initially appear supportive for a currency because stronger economic conditions may attract international investment.

However, the relationship does not end there.

As an expansion continues, businesses may find themselves competing for workers, materials, equipment, and other resources. Consumers with stronger incomes may increase spending. If demand begins growing faster than supply, inflationary pressure can develop.

The central bank may then face a different problem.

Instead of trying to encourage economic growth, policymakers may become increasingly concerned that the economy is growing too quickly and contributing to inflation.

This can lead to tighter monetary policy.

Interest rates may rise, borrowing may become more expensive, and financial conditions may gradually become more restrictive.

That means a strong economy can eventually create the conditions that contribute to slower growth.

The cycle can begin moving toward a **peak**.

A peak represents the upper portion of an economic cycle before activity begins weakening.

Identifying a peak in real time can be difficult.

Economic data does not usually announce that an economy has reached its highest point. Some indicators may remain strong while others begin deteriorating.

Employment, for example, could remain healthy even as business activity begins slowing.

Inflation might remain elevated even though consumers are becoming more cautious.

Interest rates may still be high because the central bank is attempting to control price pressures.

Forex traders therefore need to watch the direction of economic information rather than simply whether individual indicators appear strong.

Suppose GDP is still growing, but each report shows slower growth than the previous one.

PMI is declining.

Consumer confidence is weakening.

Businesses are reducing hiring.

Inflation remains high, but price pressures are beginning to ease.

The economy may still look relatively healthy when viewed through individual numbers, but the overall direction could be changing.

Eventually, an economy may enter a **contraction**, a period in which economic activity declines.

Businesses facing weaker demand may reduce production.

Investment can slow.

Hiring may decline.

Some companies may reduce their workforce.

Consumers worried about employment or financial conditions may become more cautious about spending.

These behaviors can reinforce one another.

If households spend less, businesses may experience weaker revenue. If businesses reduce hiring or employment, households may become even more cautious. Investment can decline further as companies wait for economic conditions to improve.

Central banks may begin responding as well.

If inflation is under control, policymakers may have greater flexibility to reduce interest rates or introduce other forms of monetary easing.

Expectations about those actions can affect currency markets before the policies are implemented.

Eventually, declining economic activity may reach a **trough**, the lower portion of the cycle before conditions begin improving.

Like a peak, a trough is usually easier to identify after it has occurred.

Economic conditions can still appear weak while the foundations of a recovery are developing.

Perhaps inflation has declined enough for the central bank to lower rates.

Borrowing conditions may become more supportive.

Businesses could gradually become more confident.

Consumers may begin spending more.

Production can start increasing.

The economy can then move toward another expansion.

For forex traders, the important lesson is not to attempt to identify the exact day on which an economy moves from one stage to another.

Economic cycles are not that precise.

Instead, understanding the stages provides a framework for interpreting changes in economic data and policy.

An economy moving from expansion toward contraction can produce very different expectations from one beginning to recover from a trough.

The direction matters.

Recessions, Stagflation, and Shifting Economic Conditions

A contraction can sometimes develop into a more significant economic downturn.

A **recession** generally describes a substantial decline in economic activity that spreads across the economy and lasts for a meaningful period.

During a recession, businesses may experience declining sales, investment can weaken, unemployment may rise, and consumers may reduce spending.

The specific causes can vary considerably.

An economy might enter recession after interest rates remain restrictive for an extended period.

A financial crisis could reduce lending and investment.

A major disruption to international trade could hurt businesses.

An unexpected global event might suddenly reduce economic activity.

Or several problems may occur together.

For currency traders, the economic response to a recession can be as important as the recession itself.

If inflation is relatively low, a central bank may respond to economic weakness by lowering interest rates.

Governments may also use **fiscal policy**, which refers to government spending and taxation decisions used to influence economic activity.

A government could increase spending, reduce certain taxes, or introduce other measures intended to support households and businesses.

Monetary and fiscal responses can change expectations about the future direction of the economy.

This means a currency does not necessarily continue weakening simply because current economic data is poor.

Suppose investors already expect a severe recession.

Economic data then begins showing that conditions are still weak, but not nearly as weak as anticipated.

Market expectations may improve.

Investors might begin anticipating an earlier recovery.

The currency could respond to those changing expectations even while the economy remains relatively weak.

Once again, markets can be forward-looking.

The opposite situation can occur near the end of an expansion.

Economic conditions may still appear strong, but traders could begin anticipating slower growth.

Currency markets may respond before the weakness becomes obvious in headline economic data.

Recessions can become particularly challenging when they occur alongside persistent inflation.

We introduced stagflation earlier as the combination of weak or stagnant economic growth and high inflation.

Normally, weak economic activity can give a central bank room to reduce interest rates.

But what if inflation remains extremely high?

Lowering rates could stimulate demand and potentially worsen inflation.

Keeping rates high could place additional pressure on an already weak economy.

Policymakers are faced with competing problems.

For currency traders, this creates uncertainty about both economic growth and monetary policy.

A similar conflict can occur when inflation remains high while unemployment begins increasing.

The central bank may have to decide which risk requires greater attention.

This is one reason traders should avoid treating economic indicators independently.

High inflation during a strong expansion means something different from high inflation during a recession.

Rising unemployment when inflation is low creates a different policy environment from rising unemployment when inflation remains elevated.

Economic conditions must be interpreted together.

Cycles can also be disrupted.

An economy does not always progress neatly from expansion to peak to contraction to trough.

Unexpected events can rapidly change conditions.

A supply disruption might create sudden inflation.

A financial crisis could cause investment to collapse.

A major technological development might increase productivity.

Government policy could encourage or discourage certain forms of economic activity.

International developments can affect domestic businesses and consumers.

Traders therefore use the economic-cycle framework as a guide rather than a rigid schedule.

The objective is to understand how the balance among growth, employment, inflation, and monetary policy is changing.

That balance can provide clues about where an economy may be within its cycle and how policymakers may respond.

Comparing Economic Cycles Across Countries

Economic cycles become particularly interesting for forex traders because countries do not necessarily move through them together.

One economy may be expanding while another is contracting.

One may be dealing with persistent inflation while another is experiencing weak demand.

One central bank may be raising interest rates while another is lowering them.

These differences can become important drivers of currency relationships.

Consider two hypothetical economies.

Country A is experiencing strong growth.

Unemployment is relatively low.

Business activity is expanding.

Inflation remains above the central bank's desired level.

Policymakers are discussing the possibility of maintaining higher interest rates.

Country B is experiencing a different environment.

Economic growth is weakening.

Unemployment is increasing.

Inflation has declined substantially.

Its central bank is considering lower interest rates to support the economy.

Looking at either country individually provides useful information.

Comparing them provides something more relevant to forex.

The two economies appear to be moving in different directions.

This difference is sometimes described as **economic divergence**.

Economic divergence occurs when important economic conditions or policies between countries move increasingly apart.

The opposite is **economic convergence**, in which economic conditions or policies become more similar.

Suppose both countries previously had interest rates around the same level.

Country A begins raising rates because of persistent inflation.

Country B begins cutting rates because of weak growth.

Their monetary policies are diverging.

That can change interest-rate differentials and potentially influence international capital flows.

Now imagine that several months later inflation begins falling in Country A while economic conditions improve in Country B.

Traders may begin expecting Country A to stop raising rates while Country B no longer needs additional cuts.

The outlooks are beginning to converge again.

Currency markets may respond to this changing relationship before the interest rates actually become similar.

Comparing cycles also helps explain why a seemingly weak economy can still have a relatively strong currency.

Imagine Country A is experiencing slow growth.

Viewed alone, its economic situation does not look particularly attractive.

But Country B has entered a severe recession.

When the currencies are compared, Country A may appear relatively stronger.

Forex traders therefore need to become comfortable with relative analysis.

The question is not always:

Is this economy strong?

It may be:

Is this economy becoming stronger or weaker relative to the economy on the other side of the currency pair?

That small change in perspective can make economic analysis considerably more useful.

Traders can begin by comparing the same categories across both economies.

How fast is each economy growing?

What is happening in each labor market?

Is inflation rising or falling?

What are the central banks doing?

What does the market expect them to do next?

Are business conditions improving?

Are consumers becoming more or less confident?

Where are interest-rate differentials moving?

Are international investors becoming more attracted to one economy than the other?

The answers do not automatically provide a trading decision.

They provide an economic comparison.

That comparison can then be considered alongside market expectations, price behavior, risk conditions, and the trader's broader analysis.

Timing also matters.

Two economies can eventually experience similar economic developments but reach them at different moments.

Country A may begin recovering six months before Country B.

During that period, investors may see improving opportunities in Country A while remaining cautious about Country B.

Later, Country B might begin recovering just as Country A's growth starts slowing.

The relative economic advantage has changed.

This is one reason currency relationships are dynamic.

Traders are not comparing two fixed economies.

They are comparing two economies that are continuously changing.

Economic cycles provide a way to organize those changes.

Instead of looking at GDP, inflation, employment, PMI, interest rates, and central bank policy as separate pieces of information, traders can ask what those indicators collectively suggest about the direction of each economy.

That brings together much of what we have covered so far.

Supply and demand explain the basic market mechanism.

Inflation and interest rates help explain monetary conditions.

Economic indicators help us measure what is happening.

International trade and capital flows connect economies.

Economic cycles help us understand how those conditions evolve over time.

The final step is learning how to organize this information into a practical economic framework for analyzing currencies.

Last Thoughts

Economic cycles remind forex and currency traders that economic conditions are constantly evolving. Expansion can eventually create inflationary pressures, peaks can give way to slowing activity, contractions can lead policymakers toward economic support, and troughs can eventually develop into new periods of growth. Recessions and stagflation can complicate those patterns further, particularly when policymakers must balance weak growth against persistent inflation. For forex traders, the most useful perspective comes from comparing where two economies appear to be within their cycles and whether their conditions are converging or diverging. A currency pair represents a relationship between two changing economic environments. In the next chapter, we will bring the concepts from throughout the book together and examine how traders can apply economics when comparing currencies, interpreting economic news, and making more informed trading decisions.

Chapter 6: Applying Economics to Forex and Currency Trading

Learning individual economic concepts is only the beginning. The greater challenge for forex and currency traders is learning how to connect those concepts when evaluating two currencies. Inflation, economic growth, employment, interest rates, central bank policy, international trade, and capital flows can all influence currency markets, but they rarely operate independently. Traders must also account for expectations because markets may respond to what participants believe will happen next rather than simply what is happening today. This chapter brings the concepts from throughout the book together into a practical framework for comparing currencies, interpreting economic news, and using economics to support more informed trading decisions.

Comparing the Economic Strength of Two Currencies

One of the most important ideas to carry forward from this book is that forex analysis is comparative.

A currency pair contains two currencies.

That means analyzing only one side can leave you with an incomplete picture.

Suppose you are examining two hypothetical currencies: Currency A and Currency B.

The economy behind Currency A is growing. Employment is relatively strong, inflation is declining, and its central bank is maintaining current interest rates.

At first glance, those conditions might appear favorable.

But now consider Currency B.

Its economy is growing even faster. Employment conditions are improving, inflation remains above the central bank's preferred level, and policymakers are signaling that interest rates may remain higher for longer.

Currency A may have a healthy economy, but Currency B could still appear relatively more attractive to some market participants.

This is why traders can benefit from developing a **relative economic analysis**.

Rather than asking whether an economic indicator is simply good or bad, compare similar information across the two economies represented by a currency pair.

Begin with economic growth.

Is GDP expanding in both economies?

Which economy is growing faster?

More importantly, which economy appears to be gaining momentum?

An economy growing at 3 percent but slowing may present a different outlook from one growing at 2 percent but accelerating.

Next, consider employment.

Are businesses hiring?

Is unemployment increasing or decreasing?

Are wages creating additional inflationary pressure?

Does the labor market appear resilient, or are signs of weakness beginning to emerge?

Then consider inflation.

Inflation of 3 percent in one country cannot be evaluated completely without considering inflation in the other country.

The direction matters too.

One economy could have higher inflation that is rapidly declining, while another has lower inflation that has started accelerating.

Those trends may create different expectations for monetary policy.

Interest rates provide another important comparison.

Instead of simply asking which country currently has higher rates, traders can examine how the interest rate differential is changing.

Perhaps Country A has higher rates today, but its central bank is expected to begin cutting them.

Country B has lower rates, but its central bank is expected to keep them unchanged.

The current difference may favor Country A, while expectations suggest that advantage could shrink.

Central bank policy therefore adds a forward-looking element to the comparison.

Traders can ask:

What is each central bank doing?

Why is it doing it?

What does it appear likely to do next?

How does that compare with what markets already expect?

International trade and investment can provide additional context.

An economy experiencing strong foreign investment may attract capital from abroad. An economy facing deteriorating investment conditions could experience capital moving elsewhere.

Trade conditions can affect currency demand as businesses purchase and sell products internationally.

The economic cycle can then help organize all of this information.

Perhaps one country appears to be moving through a healthy expansion while another is approaching contraction.

Perhaps both are slowing, but one is deteriorating more rapidly.

Perhaps one has already passed through a downturn and appears to be entering recovery.

There is no single economic score that combines all of these variables perfectly.

That is not the objective.

The objective is to develop a comparative picture.

A trader might conclude:

Economy A has stronger current growth.

Economy B has lower inflation.

Economy A has higher interest rates.

Economy B's central bank appears more likely to raise rates in the future.

Economy A's labor market is weakening.

Economy B's business activity is improving.

Now the trader has something more useful than an isolated economic statistic.

They have a developing economic story for each currency.

The next challenge is understanding how new information changes that story.

Reading Economic News and Market Expectations

Forex traders have access to an enormous amount of economic information.

GDP reports are released.

Inflation numbers are published.

Employment data changes.

Central bankers give speeches.

Governments announce policies.

Businesses report changing conditions.

International events affect trade and investment.

Trying to react to every headline can quickly become overwhelming.

A more useful approach is learning to distinguish between information and **market-moving information**.

Not every economic report has the same significance.

A minor data release may have little effect on expectations, while an important inflation report can cause traders to reconsider the future path of monetary policy.

An unexpected central bank announcement can change the outlook even more dramatically.

An **economic calendar** can help traders organize scheduled economic releases and policy events.

Economic calendars commonly identify upcoming reports, their scheduled release times, previous results, and forecasts or consensus expectations.

Instead of seeing an inflation report appear unexpectedly, a trader can know in advance when the report is scheduled.

Preparation matters because economic releases can sometimes produce rapid market movements.

However, knowing when a report will arrive is only the first step.

The trader still needs to understand what the report measures and why the market cares about it.

Suppose an inflation report is scheduled for Friday.

Before the release, a trader can consider several questions.

What was the previous inflation rate?

What does the market expect this time?

Has inflation recently been accelerating or slowing?

What has the central bank said about inflation?

Could a surprising result meaningfully change expectations about interest rates?

Now imagine the market expects inflation of 3 percent.

The actual report is 3.8 percent.

The important information is not simply that inflation is 3.8 percent.

The **economic surprise** is the difference between the actual result and what participants expected.

A larger-than-expected inflation reading could cause traders to reconsider whether the central bank will maintain restrictive policy for longer.

But even then, the trader should resist jumping directly from the report to a predetermined conclusion about the currency.

Perhaps other recent indicators show that the economy is rapidly weakening.

Perhaps the central bank has already indicated that it considers the inflation increase temporary.

Perhaps market participants had privately anticipated a higher number than the published consensus suggested.

Perhaps the currency had already appreciated significantly before the report because traders expected an inflation surprise.

Context remains essential.

Central bank announcements require similar analysis.

Suppose a central bank leaves interest rates unchanged.

A headline might read:

"Central Bank Holds Rates Steady."

That sounds uneventful.

But the accompanying statement could reveal that policymakers are becoming increasingly concerned about inflation and are considering additional tightening.

The interest rate did not change.

The outlook did.

Markets may respond to that new information.

This is why traders sometimes distinguish between the **headline decision** and the broader policy message.

Speeches and press conferences can matter for the same reason.

A policymaker may provide clues about how the central bank views inflation, employment, financial conditions, or economic growth.

Traders then compare those comments with previous communications.

Has the language changed?

Are policymakers more concerned about inflation?

Are they becoming more comfortable with price stability?

Are they acknowledging weakness in employment?

Are they suggesting that rates may remain unchanged for longer?

Small changes in communication can influence expectations when markets believe those changes reveal something about future policy.

Economic news should therefore be interpreted as part of an evolving narrative.

Instead of asking only, "Was this report good or bad?" ask:

What did the market expect?

What actually happened?

Does this change the economic outlook?

Does it change expectations about monetary policy?

Does it strengthen or weaken the economic case for one currency relative to the other?

That sequence of questions can make economic news considerably easier to organize.

Building Economics Into More Informed Trading Decisions

Economic analysis becomes most useful when it supports a structured decision-making process rather than encouraging traders to react impulsively to individual headlines.

The first step is establishing the broader economic environment.

Before focusing on today's report, consider what has been happening over the previous weeks or months.

Is the economy expanding or slowing?

Is inflation increasing or decreasing?

Is the labor market strengthening or weakening?

What is the central bank currently trying to accomplish?

Are interest rates expected to rise, fall, or remain relatively stable?

What is happening in the economy behind the other currency?

This creates an **economic backdrop** against which new information can be interpreted.

Suppose the broader picture shows that inflation is declining, economic growth is slowing, and employment conditions are gradually weakening.

The central bank has maintained relatively high interest rates but has started discussing the possibility of future cuts.

A single stronger-than-expected economic report appears.

Does that one report completely reverse the trend?

Possibly, but not necessarily.

The trader can ask whether the report represents a meaningful change in economic direction or simply one piece of conflicting information.

This is one reason trends can be more useful than isolated observations.

The same principle applies when several indicators begin changing together.

Imagine that PMI improves for several months.

Consumer confidence begins recovering.

Employment remains resilient.

GDP growth accelerates.

Inflation stops declining.

Central bank officials begin expressing greater concern about renewed price pressure.

Those developments collectively tell a stronger economic story than any one report could provide.

Traders can then compare that story with conditions surrounding the other currency.

This process can help form a **fundamental bias**, which is a general economic view about the relative conditions affecting a market or currency.

A fundamental bias is not a guarantee about future price movement.

It is simply an organized interpretation of the available economic information.

For example, a trader might conclude that economic conditions currently appear relatively more supportive of Currency A than Currency B.

That does not mean Currency A must appreciate immediately.

Price movements can be influenced by positioning, sentiment, unexpected news, technical factors, changing risk preferences, and information the trader has not considered.

This is where **risk management** becomes essential.

Economic analysis can help inform a trading decision, but it cannot eliminate uncertainty.

A trader can have a well-researched economic view and still be wrong.

An unexpected political event can occur.

A central bank can surprise the market.

An economic report can sharply contradict expectations.

Market sentiment can change.

The relationship between two currencies can shift.

Risk management recognizes that uncertainty is part of trading.

The purpose of studying economics is therefore not to create absolute confidence.

In many ways, good economic analysis should do the opposite.

It should make traders more aware of how many variables can affect a currency and why certainty should be approached cautiously.

A trader who understands economics can learn to think in probabilities rather than guarantees.

Instead of saying:

"This inflation report means the currency will rise."

The trader might think:

"This inflation report was higher than expected. If it changes expectations toward tighter monetary policy while the other country's outlook remains unchanged, it could create a relatively more supportive environment for this currency. But I still need to consider what the market had already priced in and what other risks are present."

That is a much more disciplined way of interpreting economic information.

It also helps prevent **confirmation bias**, which occurs when people favor information that supports what they already believe while discounting information that challenges their view.

Suppose a trader believes strongly that a currency should appreciate.

A positive GDP report supports that belief.

The trader pays close attention to it.

A weak employment report appears the following week.

The trader dismisses it.

Inflation then falls faster than expected.

The trader finds another reason to ignore that information.

Eventually, the analysis is no longer about understanding the economy.

It has become an attempt to defend an existing opinion.

A more disciplined trader should be willing to update an economic view when the evidence changes.

That does not mean changing opinions after every report.

It means recognizing when enough evidence has accumulated to challenge the original assumption.

A simple economic framework can help.

Start with growth.

Then examine employment.

Evaluate inflation.

Consider interest rates and central bank policy.

Look at trade and international investment when relevant.

Determine where each economy may be within its economic cycle.

Compare the two economies.

Then ask what the market already expects.

New economic information can be added to that framework as it becomes available.

Over time, the process becomes less about memorizing economic definitions and more about recognizing relationships.

Inflation connects to central banks.

Central banks connect to interest rates.

Interest rates connect to investment incentives.

Investment connects to capital flows.

Capital flows connect to currency demand.

Growth connects to employment.

Employment connects to wages and spending.

Trade connects economies and creates currency transactions.

Expectations connect the future to today's market prices.

These relationships are the economic foundation beneath fundamental forex analysis.

The trader's job is not to know everything.

It is to understand enough of the economic picture to make more informed decisions while recognizing that the market can always behave differently from what the analysis suggests.

Last Thoughts

Applying economics to forex and currency trading is ultimately an exercise in comparison, context, and uncertainty. A trader can compare growth, employment, inflation, interest rates, central bank policies, international flows, and economic cycles across two economies to develop a clearer understanding of the forces surrounding a currency pair. Economic news can then be evaluated according to what the market expected, what actually happened, and whether the new information meaningfully changes that broader picture. None of this provides certainty about the next exchange-rate movement, nor does economic knowledge remove the risks involved in trading. What it provides is a more structured way to interpret information. Instead of seeing currencies only as prices moving across a chart, traders can begin seeing the economies, expectations, policies, incentives, and decisions operating behind those movements.

Last Thoughts

Understanding economics does not mean knowing exactly where a currency will move next. The foreign exchange market brings together countless participants, economic conditions, policy decisions, expectations, and international transactions, all of which can change over time. What economic knowledge provides is a framework for making sense of those changes. Instead of seeing an inflation report, interest-rate decision, or GDP release as an isolated event, you can begin understanding how that information fits into a larger economic picture. The purpose of this book has been to give you that foundation so you can approach forex and currency markets with greater context and make more informed decisions.

Looking Beyond the Currency Chart

Price charts are useful tools.

They show where an exchange rate has been, how quickly it has moved, where volatility has increased or decreased, and how buyers and sellers have behaved over a particular period.

But a chart cannot tell the entire story.

Behind every currency pair are two economies.

Those economies contain consumers purchasing goods and services, businesses making investments, governments collecting and spending money, central banks setting monetary policy, exporters selling products abroad, importers purchasing foreign goods, and investors deciding where they want to place their capital.

Currency markets connect these activities.

Throughout this book, we began with the basic idea that supply and demand help determine prices in markets. In forex, those forces become particularly interesting because purchasing one currency involves exchanging another.

That creates a relative relationship.

A currency does not simply become strong.

It strengthens relative to another currency.

Likewise, economic strength is often most useful to a forex trader when it is considered comparatively.

One economy may be growing, but another could be growing faster.

Inflation may be falling in one country, but it could be falling even more rapidly somewhere else.

One central bank may have higher interest rates, but another may be preparing to raise rates while the first is preparing to lower them.

Looking beyond the chart means learning to recognize these relationships.

It also means understanding that economic information can affect currencies through multiple channels.

Inflation can influence expectations about monetary policy.

Monetary policy can influence interest rates.

Interest rates can influence borrowing, spending, and investment.

Differences in investment opportunities can influence capital flows.

International capital flows can create additional demand for currencies.

Trade creates another set of relationships as businesses exchange currencies to purchase and sell goods and services internationally.

Economic cycles change the environment surrounding all of these activities.

The result is not a simple formula.

It is an interconnected economic system.

This is why a currency can sometimes move in a direction that initially seems inconsistent with the latest economic report.

The market may have expected a different result.

Investors may be focusing on another indicator.

The economic information may already have been reflected in prices.

Conditions in the other economy may have changed.

Or traders may believe the new information will cause a central bank to respond differently in the future.

The chart shows the resulting price movement.

Economics can help you investigate the possible story behind it.

Neither should be mistaken for certainty.

A trader who learns to look beyond the chart is not trying to explain every movement perfectly. Instead, the goal is to recognize that exchange rates exist within a much larger economic environment.

That perspective can make the information surrounding forex markets easier to organize and understand.

Continuing to Build Your Economic Knowledge

The concepts introduced throughout this book provide a foundation, but economics is a much larger subject.

You do not need to master all of it before following currency markets.

A more practical approach is to continue developing your knowledge around the economic concepts that repeatedly appear in forex analysis.

Inflation is one example.

You now understand why traders monitor consumer and producer prices, but you can continue learning how inflation develops, how persistent different forms of inflation can become, and how policymakers evaluate changing price pressures.

Central banking provides another area for continued study.

Knowing that central banks can raise or lower interest rates is useful. Understanding how policymakers communicate their intentions, evaluate risks, and respond differently during various stages of an economic cycle can provide considerably more context.

International trade can be studied more deeply as well.

Trade balances, tariffs, supply chains, exchange rates, and international investment interact in complicated ways. Countries also have very different economic structures. A development that is extremely important to one economy may have a much smaller effect on another.

The same principle applies to economic indicators.

Learning what GDP, CPI, PCE, PPI, PMI, unemployment, and consumer confidence measure is the beginning.

The next step is learning how those indicators behave over time.

Rather than looking only at the latest number, observe trends.

Is inflation accelerating or decelerating?

Is economic growth gaining or losing momentum?

Is unemployment gradually increasing?

Are business conditions improving?

Are several indicators beginning to tell a similar story?

This type of observation can help transform economic data from a collection of numbers into a developing economic narrative.

It can also help you understand that the importance of different indicators changes.

During a period of unusually high inflation, inflation reports and central bank communications may receive exceptional attention.

During a recession, employment and growth indicators may become increasingly important.

During a major international trade dispute, tariffs and trade information may receive greater attention.

The market's focus can shift because the economic problem receiving the most attention can shift.

Continuing your economic education therefore involves more than learning additional definitions.

It means learning how to ask better questions.

What is the most important economic issue affecting this country right now?

What is its central bank trying to accomplish?

Which indicators are providing evidence about whether those policies are working?

How are expectations changing?

How does this economy compare with the economy behind the other currency?

Those questions can guide further learning without requiring you to study every branch of economics at once.

You can gradually build your knowledge as you encounter new situations.

The objective is not to reach a point where there is nothing left to learn.

Markets and economies continuously provide new circumstances to study.

The objective is to develop a foundation strong enough that new information has somewhere to fit.

Becoming a More Informed Currency Market Participant

Being informed does not mean being certain.

That distinction may be one of the most important lessons in this book.

A trader can carefully analyze inflation, employment, GDP, interest rates, monetary policy, trade, capital flows, and economic cycles and still reach a conclusion that the market does not ultimately support.

Economic relationships are complicated.

Expectations change.

Unexpected events occur.

Other market participants may interpret the same information differently.

This is why economic knowledge should support disciplined decision-making rather than excessive confidence.

One of the risks traders face is **overconfidence bias**, the tendency to overestimate the accuracy of one's own knowledge, judgment, or abilities.

Learning more about economics can ironically make this risk more important.

Once you understand why higher interest rates can attract capital, for example, it can become tempting to assume that you know exactly how a currency should respond to an interest-rate increase.

But you also need to consider inflation.

Growth.

Expectations.

The other currency.

Future central bank policy.

Market positioning.

Risk sentiment.

And the possibility that the relationship you expect simply does not dominate the market at that moment.

Economic knowledge is most valuable when it helps you recognize complexity rather than ignore it.

The same applies to confirmation bias, which we discussed in the previous chapter.

A trader should be willing to reconsider an economic view when the evidence changes.

Suppose you believe one economy is strengthening relative to another.

At first, the evidence supports your view.

Growth is improving.

Employment is strong.

The central bank appears concerned about inflation.

Then conditions begin changing.

Business activity weakens.

Employment growth slows.

Inflation falls faster than expected.

Central bank officials become less concerned about price pressures.

An informed market participant should be willing to recognize that the original economic story may no longer apply.

Changing your analysis when the evidence changes is not a failure.

It is part of analyzing a changing economy.

This is also why risk management remains important regardless of how convincing an economic argument appears.

No economic thesis eliminates uncertainty.

Instead, the concepts throughout this book can help you approach that uncertainty with more context.

When you see an inflation report, you can consider what it might mean for purchasing power and monetary policy.

When interest rates change, you can consider how the decision affects borrowing, investment incentives, and interest-rate differentials.

When GDP or employment data is released, you can think about where the economy may be within its economic cycle.

When tariffs or trade policies change, you can consider how businesses, consumers, imports, exports, and international investment might respond.

When analyzing a currency pair, you can compare these conditions across both economies.

And when the market reacts differently from what you expected, you can ask why instead of immediately assuming the market is wrong.

That curiosity is valuable.

Every economic release becomes an opportunity to strengthen your understanding of how markets process information.

Over time, the terminology that once seemed complicated can become easier to recognize. Economic reports can become easier to place within context. Central bank decisions can become easier to connect with inflation and growth. Currency movements can become easier to examine as part of relationships between economies.

You may still not know where the market will move next.

No economic framework can guarantee that.

But you can understand more about the environment in which that movement is occurring.

Last Thoughts

Forex and currency markets provide a real-world example of how deeply connected the global economy has become. Exchange rates reflect more than trading activity alone. They exist within a larger system shaped by supply and demand, inflation, interest rates, central banks, economic indicators, international trade, capital flows, economic cycles, expectations, and human decision-making. Becoming more informed means learning to connect these forces without assuming that any single indicator can provide certainty about what happens next. Continue studying the economies behind the currencies, continue comparing conditions rather than examining them in isolation, and continue allowing new evidence to challenge your assumptions. The more clearly you understand the economic forces surrounding a currency market, the better prepared you can be to interpret what you see and approach your decisions with greater context and discipline.

About the Author

Roggie "Raj" Clark is an entrepreneur and a 10-year marketing professional with a proven track record in e-commerce and digital business growth. Having built and managed successful online stores with thousands of sales and consulted for numerous marketing clients, Roggie has mastered the intricacies of online marketing, branding, and consumer behavior. He has also written several popular books on digital marketing, SEO (search engine optimization), and programming (HTML, CSS, and JavaScript).

As a former marketing manager at a fintech company—a role he secured through his own marketing and financial expertise—Roggie gained firsthand experience in financial strategy and wealth-building. This journey inspired him to share insights with amateur investors, helping them save money, make smarter financial decisions, and build long-term wealth. Raj currently lives in Maryland with his sister and niece.

www.ingramcontent.com/pod-product-compliance
Lightning Source LLC
LaVergne TN
LVHW050823061126
851857LV00012B/943